JOEL FINE, MD

Arc of
the Covenant

A PSYCHIATRIST TRACKS
HIS PATH IN JUDAISM

Table of Contents

Arc of the Covenant

Introduction

My journey in Yiddishkeit began a long, long time ago. Arguably, since I have a Jewish neshama, or soul, I was present in some form at Mount Sinai for the giving of the Ten Commandments and Torah. I don't have an independent recollection.

Representing a fraction of the world population for thousands of years, and faced with persecution, forced conversion, intermarriage, and secularization, it is remarkable that our collective Jewish identity persists in our predominantly non-Jewish world. How have we managed to survive? It seems to me that there must be something at our core—whether it is the beliefs that we share or, in fact, our neshamas—something has persisted that has kept us going. It also seems reasonable to conclude that more strict observance has been required over the generations to perpetuate Judaism as we know it.

Why are some Jews so much more observant than others, with the range being from not identifying yourself as Jewish to practicing the tenets of our faith as Jews have done for hundreds of generations? There might well be as many answers as there are individual circumstances. What I intend to do is follow the arc that I have taken toward a more observant lifestyle. It's my hope that other Jews might become a bit more comfortable with the import and usefulness of these choices, and become more observant themselves.

I'd like to believe that if you are Jewish, or your mother was Jewish, or your mother's mother's mother's mother all the way back to the time of Sinai was Jewish, and you are currently not observant, then this book is for you. If you are observant, or even not Jewish, it might be worth your perusal, since I occasionally say funny things and have some reasonable insights about how things fit together.

The Arc

Rabbi Yisroel ben Eliezer, also known as the Baal Shem Tov, one of the holiest, most spiritual Jews of all time, was reportedly aware of his conception. I can't lay claim to that, but I could ask my folks about what they remember.

As a psychiatrist, it's part of my job, and it's inherent in the personality of many of us to question and challenge and ponder the veracity of thoughts and ideas. Questioning, challenging, and thinking are common Jewish traits. We don't have a monopoly on these characteristics, but we can certainly lay claim to more than a fraction of 1 percent of the world's ambivalence. Being more observant now, I still wonder about the sanctity of my convictions, but I am more convinced of them. Here, I intend to trace over the path my life has taken, try and make sense of my increased observation of Judaism, talk like a psychiatrist, and try to be moderately entertaining. We will see what happens.

Back to conception. Traditional or orthodox Jews tend to believe that whether or not you're Jewish is completely dependent on whether or not your mother was Jewish. (Or if you have had a halachic conversion). That's not the case at the other end of the Judaic spectrum. I recall from a course that my wife and I took together before we got married a Reform rabbi incredulously asking, "Do you think there is a little Star of David on the sperm or the egg?" Suffice it to say, all available evidence seems to point to me being Jewish. I do have a Jewish mother. I had a bris when I was eight days old. I was told it didn't hurt, but like the old joke goes, I was not able to walk for a year after that. I recall seeing grainy film of my Pidyon Haben, or "redemption of the firstborn," where my dad bought me for some silver dollars.

So I'm in this world, in a Jewish home. My earliest memory is square dancing at preschool. What I remember distinctly is my partner poking me in the eye. I also remember *thinking* that she was going to poke me in the eye. Now why would she do that? And why does that have to be my earliest memory? Well, I believe the preschool was at a Jewish community center. The poke in the eye might have been the genesis of my drift away from Judaism.

I have several, actually quite a few, memories from kindergarten. I remember getting beat up one day walking home from school. That fits very nicely with a recurring theme in my collective remembrances. I do remember waiting outside of class for it to begin on the first day…no association or recollection of getting hurt. Hooray! My earliest Jewish memories are of the separate dishes my mom put out for Friday night dinner. I've seen the film of lighting Hanukkah candles as a little kid, but I have no other independent recollections from way back then.

The Reform synagogue that my parents belonged to in San Diego had a rabbi, but no building. When I was six or so, the synagogue merged with another group that had a building, but no rabbi. I remember attending Hebrew school once a week and religious school on Saturday mornings.

We had a bit of a drive to get there. Nobody else from my public school went there. I had a friend, another kid that we carpooled with, but for the most part, I was a bit outside of the group at religious school. This Jewish stuff was certainly cutting into my athletic endeavors. Little League baseball, and then basketball starting when I was ten, was invariably centered on Saturday games. My mom was working on her PhD in Jewish studies. Her curriculum did not seem to intersect much with mine. My father is very proud of his Jewish heritage, and though he was not active with ritual practice, led Friday night blessings over the wine and did his share of driving back and forth to synagogue. Hebrew and religious school were interfering with my friendships from public school and what I wanted to be doing with my time. We kept doing those Friday night dinners and sometimes schlepping off to synagogue for Friday night services. I maintained a very strong Jewish identity. Why and how was this the case? Some quality psychobabble is that the successful resolution of an oedipal complex for a boy includes strong identification with his father. That certainly fits with the fact that I became a doctor like my dad, and I am also off to the right somewhere politically. With a felt pen I wrote "Israel must live" on the wallet I had made in Cub Scouts. Yet at the same time I was asking, contemplating, and certainly whining and complaining about why I needed to go to religious school. Churning, folding, and stirring the above ingredients—the lack of connection to religious school classmates, missing sports activities back home, and not much practice of Judaism besides Shabbat dinner—laid the foundation for the normal development of an agnostic teenager.

So on one hand, I had a clear Jewish identity; on the other hand, it didn't make a lot of sense to me what I should do with it. A common way to deal with ambivalence of any kind is to talk about it out loud. I was a reasonably intelligent and verbal kid. Thus, I loved to argue and debate in a competitive way. The issues of religion, God, evolution, et al., were perfect fodder. All the pontificating I did worked out for the most part socially and scholastically, although my mom did call me a male chauvinist pig on more than one occasion. Today, she says she never did, which is nice to know.

The active Christian youth movements at my public high school, which were pervasive enough to include prayers in the huddle before basketball games, didn't seem to have too much of an effect on me. I was accepting of others, and my gentile friends were universally okay with me being Jewish. There were certainly attempts by some in my high school to get me more involved with the Christian activities. When I first made the varsity basketball team, the charismatic team captain tried to convert me, like he had others. A handful of my friends were active in Christian retreats and routinely invited me to join them. I don't recall ever being ostracized because I did not drift more toward the mean. As an aside, it surprised me that when I went back down to San Diego for my twentieth high school reunion, several of my old classmates went out of their way to tell stories of how they had met and become friends with other Jews. A typical one was a girl who went to school in New Jersey, and she related she had no idea there were so many other Jews out there. I was the only one that she had known. I did not experience or believe that I was anything special for others because I was Jewish, but years later it seems to be that this was the case. I think Gentiles want Jews to be Jews.

For college, I loaded my car and headed up the road to UCLA, taking my Jewish identity and right-wing politics with me. It's kind of funny to me when I look back at it, but in a political science class my freshman year when the professor shared the statistic that two-thirds of Jews were liberals, I couldn't believe it! I thought all Jews were conservatives. I guess I was somewhat sheltered. Commensurate with this, I seemed to be fine with the fact I didn't have much observance of Jewish ritual or practice. Soon after school started, Yom Kippur was upon us. I recall a conversation with my mom. She was interested and curious what my plans would be. She wanted me to attend High Holiday services. I told her that I had looked them up and found out that there would be services at a Jewish community center in Santa Monica on Wilshire Boulevard.

Let me digress. Today, when I get lost or make a wrong turn, my wife affectionately calls me "Wrong Way Feldman." My paternal grandmother

Rose, who was instrumental in my life in many ways, once told me that she always left the house early, since she knew she was going to get lost. I incorporated her habit and style, which has allowed me to stay relatively calm and not panic when I don't have a clue of where I am…which happens a bunch. So much so that a few years back when I called from Monterey and reported to my wife I was lost, again, she had heard enough. She bought me a Garmin and told me to plug it in.

There was no such thing as GPS in '78. And I did not know that you were supposed to turn right on Wilshire Boulevard to go to Santa Monica. Once I turned left, the street numbers started getting smaller, which is what I needed to happen. Well, actually, I guess not, since I was going the wrong way. I was new to LA, so passing through Beverly Hills didn't mean anything to me. It did mean something when I was in downtown Los Angeles, and the address I needed didn't seem to exist. It was also clear by the time I made my way back up Wilshire Boulevard that I was not going to make it to services. This level of commitment, observance, and devotion was maintained through college and into medical school.

In fact, the extent to which I was oblivious to Jewish life on campus is striking. UCLA had one of the largest Hillel organizations anywhere. I did not attend a single event. And it was several years back while visiting Chabad of California on Gayley Avenue that I read about how the building had burned down in 1980, and several young men lost their lives. My apartment at the time was a quarter of a mile away from that site, and I was not aware of this tragic event until my visit.

In med school, several of my close friends were Mormon. I was a clean-cut, well behaved kid, and it was apparent to many that I was also Mormon. I relished those friendships as well as the opportunities to be one of the three non-Mormon ringers the Mormon basketball league teams were allowed. That was probably the best basketball team I ever played on. We won a regional championship, which in past years would have earned a trip to Salt Lake City if they were still doing their national tournament.

I was comfortable with who I was. It didn't seem like a big deal to stand to the side while my teammates prayed together in the center of the court, despite what I thought others would think about this, or how it might appear. At the same time, I was apparently not oblivious to my heritage away from the court. A close friend affectionately called me "Rabbi," and I did host a seder in my apartment one year for several of my friends, yet I don't believe I ever went to synagogue in Washington DC, nor did I date a Jewish girl during my four years there.

I moved to Denver for my residency. It was there I met my dear wife, Kelly. It was about five months into my internship there, while doing a neurology rotation, that I first laid eyes on her. I will save my opening lines for another story, another day. Suffice it to say, after we had dated for ten months, we were talking seriously about marriage.

Kelly reminds me that I told her I wanted to raise our children Jewish. I recall letting her know that I was fine whether or not she converted; I still wanted to marry her. I made the suggestion of an introduction to Judaism course to help clue her in on some traditions. It seemed reasonable that I would take it with her. It was a six-month course covering the holidays, birth, marriage, death, and a variety of other topics. Most of the way through the course, it occurred to her that she wanted to convert to Judaism. Similar to her experience, I felt more connected and interested in being involved in the practice of Judaism. We still have the book that we used and shared for that class. Picking it up now, a couple things are readily apparent based on all the notes we each took. First, there was a lot that each of us learned. Second, her handwriting is way better than mine.

Our first Passover together, I put on a seder for just the two of us. It's interesting to realize that the Passover seder seemed to survive the nadirs of my Jewish observance. In a recent lecture, Rabbi Y. Y. Jacobson identified circumcision and the Passover seder as the two ritual observances that routinely transcend assimilation. My Passover seders away from home might not have been completely kosher, but I did hide the afikomen, which Kelly was able to find against no competition. Her prize: an 8×10 picture of me!

We began going to services regularly on Friday nights at Temple Emanuel in Denver and became dues-paying members. We met with Rabbi Foster there about conversion, and he gave Kelly a list of ten things that he expected from his converts. One of them was to make some type of dietary concession consistent with kosher laws. Kelly took that one plus the other nine and did quite well with them. I, on the other hand, struggled mightily with the food thing. I reconciled my difficulty by deciding not to eat meat and milk together except for pepperoni pizza. Man is highly adaptable but resistant to change.

When we moved to Vacaville in 1990, we discovered there was a Jewish community held together with scotch tape. It was a nice group of folk who occasionally would hold a service led by a layperson in the chapel at Travis Air Force Base. I remember a pool party at the home of Lois and Harvey Kaplow, long-standing residents and members of the community. Harvey was telling me that since we were young, we would probably move on to the synagogue in Vallejo, since they had a building, a part-time rabbi, and more to offer. "Nah," I said to Harvey. "We'll probably stay right here with this group." Turns out Harvey had wisdom to match his prescience. We started going to the Vallejo about a month later.

It was about that time that Rabbi David Kopstein, who would later become one of my best buddies, was negotiating with that synagogue to become its full-time rabbi. I'm sure that it was mainly because of him that we made a nice connection with the whole setup there. We went to Saturday morning services on regular basis and did some social stuff with the community. Services on Saturday morning were not that well attended, which made it a bit easier for Rabbi David to hold Samantha, our first kid, in his arms up on the bimah when he would lead the Shema.

Rabbi Kopstein led the service at our home for the baby naming of Carolyn, kid number two. I remember that he inspired me in many ways. When he would pray, sing, or teach, he would resonate a spirituality that I aspired to reach. He was not strictly observant in a literal sense, but he was certainly a role model for me to do more myself, keeping in mind the path I have taken has not been a bullet train ride to orthodoxy. I recall asking him if it was okay to mow the lawn and do yard work on Shabbat. I reasoned out loud that it was not my normal work, and in fact I enjoyed it. He did not condone it, but I also didn't hear a "no," so I was okay doing what I was doing. It might've been around that time that I became active on the synagogue board. Oy. Actually things weren't too bad for a while, but there was political stuff and money issues that started to mount until the big one came. By a five to four vote, the board decided to ask Rabbi Kopstein to take a $2000 pay cut. This didn't make a lot of sense to me, or to him—surprise, surprise—considering that we had almost $100,000 in the bank. It was a slow-moving disaster, and it wasn't difficult to foresee that Rabbi Kopstein wouldn't be able to stay at the synagogue with this new financial paradigm. When he left, so did we. For better or worse, our connection to him was much stronger than it was to the community or the building.

It was around this time that we stepped up the level of our kosher observance. My wife made the decision that we were going to now have separate dishes for meat and milk. Commensurate with this higher level of observance for dietary laws, we were prepared to check out conservative synagogues. I would be the scout. It was my duty to go ahead of the family and seek out the new synagogue or Jewish community. This time I headed east, fifty minutes from Vacaville toward Sacramento to Mosaic Law Congregation. The building and physical plant were nice. There was wonderful singing and spirit on this particular Shabbos. I enjoyed the community feel and my introduction to Rabbi Taff. What really sold me was the talk that I had with his wife, Judy, that day. She was running the school at the time. I told her about our situation in Vacaville, about our kids and their ages. She was struck by how far we would be driving on a regular basis. I can't remember exactly what she said, but what came across was a remarkable regard for myself and our situation. I remember having some tears in my eyes (keeping in mind that I cry at the end of the *Star Trek* movie every time Mr. Spock dies—and frankly I cry at just about every movie I ever see—still take it as a given that what she said was quite touching and supportive). So I returned home, gave my report, and off we went to our new synagogue on a regular basis.

Early on Rabbi Taff gave a sermon where he talked about two young Israeli entrepreneurs who had been very successful with a software program. A key point he made was that they were proud of themselves and their accomplishment. He was struck that they did not thank God for their success. I was struck by the thought of why in the world would they need to thank God for their accomplishments.

Very straightforward: they worked hard, and they had gotten ahead. The key word being the third-person plural pronoun "they," not God.

In another sermon he introduced me to the word "gematria." He explained that each Hebrew word had a numerical value, since Hebrew letters are also numbers. Looking at the numerical value of words or even sentences allows someone to make connections between words, sentences, or concepts. I have absolutely no idea what this particular example was, but I was struck by what a bunch of hooey it was. It seemed straightforward that you would be able to make stuff like this up—not the numerical value itself, but you would be able to make any point you wanted by picking and choosing words with different numerical values. That's where I was at the time with Rabbi Taff's ideas about things.

Besides these intellectual challenges, a social one came up when Kelly and I met with him to talk about membership, and he shared with us his visions for his synagogue. He had it clear in his mind that he wanted Mosaic Law to be more like a center of Jewish activities. He envisioned a much larger physical plant with a bigger school and community center. He talked about the importance of living in the Jewish community and encouraged us to look into moving closer.

That concept made a lot of sense to my wife, who has always been a tad ahead of me in understanding the important aspects of Jewish life. Being in my thirties and never having lived in a Jewish community like the one Rabbi Taff envisioned, it just didn't make that much sense to me—especially when considering my private practice was growing roots in Vacaville. A practical issue was what I would do with my business if we moved. Suffice it to say, we actively looked into it, but after weighing out everything, we decided to stay put. So we continued driving to Sacramento routinely on Shabbos, for religious school on Sunday, and then once or twice a week for Hebrew school.

Meanwhile, another conservative rabbi was trying to set up camp in Vacaville. Rabbi Vale had been at Travis Air Force Base in Fairfield, the next closest town, and had been meeting with members of the local group and a few others to assess the possibility of making a go of it in Solano County. Rabbi Vale and I had a very pleasant lunch. He seemed to appreciate that we were integrated into the school system in Sacramento. For a period of time it didn't make sense to switch our allegiance.

Though the school of Mosaic Law in Sacramento was top-notch and the rabbi was wonderful, we did not do a good job of socially integrating into the community. We were outsiders. We did not receive invitations to other families' homes, but then again, we were also not making additional trips to Sacramento for various synagogue activities besides religious services and school. On the other hand, back in our ol' hometown, Rabbi Vale had coalesced a group of about forty families into a community. As Samantha was nearing bat mitzvah age, we made the decision to put our energy and financial support behind the local congregation, Ha Makom.

2

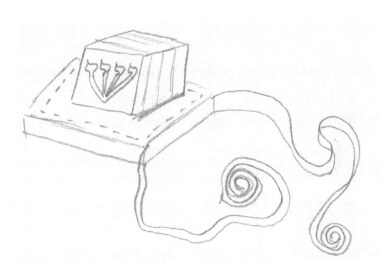

The move back home brought with it a closer and more intimate connection with our rabbi. Besides being more accessible for questions and discussion, a rabbi of a small group will have more of a direct effect on his congregants. For me, the result was the decision to purchase my first pair of tefillin.

I talked to Rabbi Vale about what to get and how much to spend. I shopped around online and was overwhelmed with the number of choices and options. Not being a sophisticated tefillin shopper, I bought mine on eBay. For Jewish men, there is nothing that quite binds you to daily Jewish ritual than putting on tefillin every morning. Once I had my very own tefillin, I began to pray religiously, so to speak, every a.m. In fact, since I got my tefillin, only one day has passed that I didn't put them on and do at least some of the morning prayer service. That would have been on September 11, 2005. On that day I woke up especially early to go help set up a garage sale for the congregation. After a couple hours there, I went home and got ready quickly so I could meet my friend Dr. Larry Corman for a morning bike ride. During that ride I fell and fractured two ribs, punctured a lung, and broke my clavicle, which eventually required surgery to repair. Dr. Corman flipped over the top of me and did not fare much better.

As human beings, we have a penchant for discerning meaning in just about anything. *Hashgacha Pratis* is a term that means divine providence. Stuff happens, and it's always for a reason. Through the process of becoming more observant, I have experienced many events, moments, and perceptions that help me understand God's hand in everyday life. This particular smackdown was a clear message to not forget to put on tefillin every morning.

There was a write up in the local newspaper when Samantha became the first bat mitzvah in Vacaville history. I became active with the board, and we were as close to the Jewish community as we had ever been. We had a really nice run with our local group. Eventually, though, a headwind was stirred up by personality conflicts and institutional angst. It was different, though, from when we were in Vallejo. We were also evolving ourselves and becoming a bit more observant. I was putting on tefillin, studying the weekly parsha, and doing a better job with kosher dietary laws. Long gone was the pepperoni pizza, but we were still okay eating at nonkosher restaurants. We were taking our Judaism seriously in such a way that we needed more. Sparing you the details of the last straw, shortly after Carolyn's bat mitzvah it was time to send the scout out in search of a new Jewish home.

This time I went west, just under an hour to an Orthodox synagogue in Berkeley. We knew about this shul because my second cousin Shelly had been going there for years and spoke of it very highly. It definitely helped having someone I knew show me the ropes of a different prayer service. My first Shabbos in Berkeley I was duly impressed by the tremendous spirit and warmth from the community. I reported back to the family, and the following sentence can be sung to the *Beverly Hillbillies* theme song: So we loaded up the car and drove to Berkeley...Orthodox...mechitza...different.

The mechitza is what seems to freak most Jews out when they attend an Orthodox service. My wife will tell you that I was no different. It's the barrier between the men's and women's sections. In a small shul, it's usually portable. In a larger one, it is often placed upstairs, with a separate physical entrance. The women in my family adapted to it quickly and easily. They told me at the time that it was something they appreciated. It took a tad for me to get used to. I missed being able to yap and poke during services. This is essentially the essence of why there is a mechitza. Maintaining concentration and focus during prayer is hard enough in and of itself without the inevitable distractions that come from mixing males and females. I'm sure there is a connection between how much of an adjustment needs to be made and who is going to benefit the most from having it there in the first place.

At this point both girls were doing some learning on their own. We were all becoming more active in our individual prayers and clearly making more of a connection to ritual law. It follows that this would occur from being involved with an Orthodox community. In addition to the mechitza, there were hints and clues for us as to what was entailed in traditional Jewish observance. They didn't have regular rolls of toilet paper at this place, rather pre cut. This was so you didn't have to tear on Shabbos. The reason for this is that tearing is one of the thirty-nine types of work forbidden on Shabbos. The thirty-nine, and their many subtypes, correspond to the thirty-nine types of work used to build the tabernacle by the Jews in the desert. We also bore witness to the fact that many people walked to synagogue on Shabbos. Lighting a fire is one of the thirty-nine; hence, igniting the spark necessary to start a car is not permitted. Walking the fifty miles to Berkeley seemed a tad too much to take on.

I'm not sure what the following story is an example of. Kelly is kind enough to say that it reflects how deep my connection is to my Jewish past. During one Shabbat service, I got up in the middle to go to the restroom. I took off my tallit and set it on the table nearby. When I came out, it was gone. I went into sheer panic mode. It was a special tallit, the one given to me on my bar mitzvah. I looked everywhere, and even considered the possibility someone had come in through the open main door and removed it. It was, of course, also possible that a latecomer had seen it and thought it was for use by the community. I tried to be unobtrusive and walked up and down the aisle looking for it on the shoulders of my fellow congregants, but to no avail. I tapped the congregation president on the shoulder and told him of the situation. He was kind enough to announce to the entire group that someone had picked up my tallit and its special significance. It actually took five to ten minutes before someone else noticed it on an elderly gentleman who did not realize what was happening. The tallit was returned to me, met with extreme relief. Whew!

When services were over, Kelly came from the women's side. I expected her to share my sense of solace and satisfaction. Instead she looked at me like I was from outer space and said, "That's not your bar mitzvah tallit; I gave that to you!"

We got an invitation or two to people's homes. We were still the outsiders, but there was no question that this was a very nice community. Commensurate with our level of observance, we thought becoming members might facilitate our further growth and development in Judaism and also integrate us further into the congregation. The four of us went to meet with the rabbi, who was at that time making plans to move to Israel. He was a remarkably kind man, but he gave us the absolutely mind-blowing news that the girls and my wife were not considered Jewish. In fairness to him, he didn't slam us, and from a halachic perspective, it was a no-brainer. But for us, considering our level of observance, the fact the girls had known only Judaism, and that my wife had gone through a conversion, it was a shock to say the least.

We decided to roll with the punches and continued attending there with the fantasy that things might change when the new rabbi arrived. So, as it turns out, three thousand years of Jewish law does not change when you get a new rabbi.

With things as they were in Berkeley, it was easier at that time to make another change. Looking back, it seems events fell into place because God planned it that way. Notice, please, that this is a different way for me to understand things than when I was at the

Mosaic Law and contemplated Rabbi Taff's sermons. My brother, who lives in Pleasanton, told me there was a new rabbi there he thought I should meet. My brother was active in his Reform congregation and had met Rabbi Resnick from Chabad, but he was not interested in becoming affiliated there. So the scout got into his car and drove one hour to the southwest to meet this new guy.

Raleigh Resnick and his wife, Fruma, had been in Pleasanton a little over a year. The first Shabbat service I spent with them, there might have been only three or four other people in attendance. They were both very accessible. I was struck by how remarkably gracious and kind they both were. It was also quite apparent that he had a three-thousand-watt brain. He talked faster than I did, and he was himself remarkably warm and gracious. And boy, oh boy, did he know his stuff, and by the way, have I told you how warm and gracious he and his wife were?

So I reported back to the family, and we started driving to Pleasanton for Shabbos. We had the hang of the mechitza. The intimacy of the small group was really neat. We had experienced that with our local group, but missed it somewhat at the larger synagogue in Berkeley. And holy Moses, did this guy know his stuff. And have I told you how warm and gracious they were?

Since there wasn't a minyan, we would usually sit around and study the week's portion during our Shabbat service in place of an actual Torah reading. One day Rabbi Resnick explained the timeline that included the Jews leaving Egypt, the fifty days until Mount Sinai, the episode of the golden calf, three forty-day time periods up and down the mountain for Moses, and how all this fits on the Jewish calendar. This blew me away. I had to call him after Shabbos to go over it again so I could write it down. This was significant for me. It was the first concrete example I can think of where what was written in the Torah could be taken to be literally true. I had always been of the impression that dates, events, and even the people mentioned in the Bible were allegorical. I was familiar with the story of the Exodus, but I had no idea that the storyline fit the calendar precisely. This was an important concept for my formerly agnostic, I-believe-in-evolution, is-there-a-God brain to chew on.

Let me go back just a tad. Some time while we were still at Mosaic Law, we attended the engagement party of Rabbi David's son Tal. It was from him that I learned something that in retrospect seems to be a foundation for my current level of observance.

Tal had become a black hat—a completely observant Jew—something neither he nor his father had seen happening a few years before. I thought that his journey was fascinating, and I was curious as to what prompted it. I don't recall the question specifically, but I asked him to explain something about his beliefs, and he responded in a remarkably succinct fashion: "It all depends on what you think happened at Sinai."

Here's what that means. If you think that the Sinai story and the giving of the Ten Commandments is something crafted a ways back, by some unknown author—maybe even more than one—it goes to follow that Reform Judaism makes sense from a historical standpoint. I expect that it would be a common belief in conservative shuls that it is not clear exactly what happened at Mount Sinai. Maybe it did happen the way it's written in the Bible, maybe not. We can't be absolutely sure. But at the other end of the spectrum, if you buy into the idea that it happened like the book said, with the thunder, smoking mountain, etc., then it wouldn't be much of a leap to buy into the rest of it—that God wrote the Torah, and all the rules and regulations that go with it.

My comfort level with the literal translation and understanding of the good book has evolved commensurate with my level of observance of the mitzvoth. Back in my college days, I can remember arguing in a debate that God did not exist. I called myself an agnostic for many years. I loved my anthropology class and asked lots of questions about evolution and ate it all up. I certainly have had lots of training in the sciences. Reconciling my religious beliefs with my educational background was made easier when I recognized that with as much study and research as there is about evolution, there still is no simple experiment with bacteria, fruit flies, or the like where any type of environmental change over a period of time has resulted in a change in species. It helps me that nothing has been shown to contradict the biblical narrative, including the story of creation. If you take it as a given that it happened just like it says in Genesis, you realize carbon dating doesn't make any sense. We certainly have no clue as to what would happen to radioactive isotopes if the Big Bang happened only 5,773 years ago. Similarly, when you create a whole big universe all at once, it makes sense that there are trees already in the ground. Those trees would have rings in their trunks indicative of a seeming paradox which shows evidence of being older than they could possibly be. This is a first cousin to the "what about the fossils" question. I have no idea about the fossils. Nor do I completely get the concept of an ostrich or a rutabaga. I do know that the questions themselves are more important than the answers.

A Kabbalist might tell you that as long as you keep asking questions, your path will become clearer. I think it's great that some of the latest stuff with string theory begs for the understanding of the old adage, the more you know, the more you know you don't know. With that in mind, it has been startling for me to see that answers that fit perfectly with cosmic questions and dilemmas are readily available with a deeper understanding of the written and oral law of Torah.

Back to Rabbi Resnick. At the same time that he couldn't have been more accepting of who we were, where we had been, and what we were doing, he and his wife were role modeling what complete Jewish observance was about. The cornerstone of Judaism—that you should love your fellow Jew as yourself—was routinely exemplified by both him and his wife. It was in this context that he told me early in our relationship that he would like nothing better than to not see me anymore on Shabbos. He wanted all the best for me and family, which included becoming more observant and no longer driving on the Sabbath. After he told me that, we continued to come regularly and increase our studies and ritual observance in other ways. I was now routinely praying three times a day.

About four years ago, he called me at the office with the most remarkable news. A young couple from Crown Heights was coming to check out Vacaville and Solano County as a possible place to settle and open another Chabad. We were thrilled. I eagerly met with Chaim and Aidel Zaklos and tried to balance my role as a source of information about the community, so they might have good data to help them make the most significant decision of their young lives, with my instinct to get on my knees and beg them to stay. The good news is that they decided to stay in Vacaville; I retained a modicum of dignity, and we stopped driving on Shabbos.

About fifteen to twenty years ago, we went to the house of a sister of one of my college classmates during Sukkot. She had converted to Judaism and married an Orthodox man, and they were living an observant life. It was hard for me then to understand how she had made such a significant transition. She explained to me that it was like a spiral: you gradually moved up, in no particular straight line, and took on more of the rituals and lifestyle gradually over time. The "spiral" is a good illustration to understand the changes we have made as a family.

Consistent with the above, and even though we already had a kosher kitchen (at least we thought so), we made the decision to step it up another level. It should not surprise the reader that there is kosher, and then there is kosher. What else is new? Rabbi Zaklos was kind enough to devote significant hours taking a blowtorch to the oven and stove and helping us prepare to tovil.

Toviling is where you take a new or freshly koshered utensil, which means it has been dipped in boiling water, to a mikveh, or fresh body of water. Now, it's not just any fresh body of water. There are rules, mind you. Rabbi Zaklos spent time on the phone with city engineers making sure that the stream where we are planning to take the dishes (since we were not near a mikveh or an ocean) would have running water throughout the year. You can't use a seasonal creek. The good news was that there was such a creek under a bridge just two miles from where we lived in out in the country. The bad news—well, do I really need to explain that this was not going to be an easy task?

So with two full carloads of dishes, utensils, and assorted kitchen accoutrements, I left the house with the rabbi, Kelly, and the girls...and a-toviling we went.

We parked along the side of the road, and it was primarily Rabbi Zaklos who carried baskets and boxes down a very steep embankment to the stream. Samantha and I would dip the item, repackage it, and give it back to the rabbi to schlep up the hill. Kelly and Carolyn were simultaneously unloading and loading up the cars. Things were going along fairly smoothly—albeit I could easily imagine Rabbi Zaklos falling and tumbling into the stream with dishes flying everywhere—until...the sheriff came.

Samantha and I were not aware of it, but apparently they asked the rabbi what was going on, and his explanation earned him a full body frisk. Rabbi Zaklos was told to sit over by the side of the road and not move. One of the officers came partway down the hill and demanded that I come up. So I struggled up the hill and was greeted by two sheriff's deputies, one of whom had his hand resting on his holster. Fortunately for the home team, I have a bit more of the gift of gab than my learned rabbi. I was able to explain the situation in such a way that I thought it was then entirely appropriate to smile and ask them if they wanted to help us. One of them was amused, the other one wasn't.

So it is now my regular practice that after we buy a new dish or utensil and I go to tovil, I call the dispatcher at the sheriff's office and explain whom I am and what is going on. Since that time, there have been no problems with the law, only dirt, mud, and the prickly vines of wild blackberries.

In a larger Jewish community, you should expect to find a full range of services that make being observant easier or more straightforward. Besides a much easier way to tovil, buy appropriate clothes (especially for girls), and pray with a minyan, there is the kosher food situation. The closest kosher restaurant to us is over an hour away. However, I think it's reasonable to conclude that God keeps track of us out here as well and wherever we go. (I want to tell you a story about that in a second). All of us, though, thoroughly enjoy our trips to Jewish communities in Los Angeles and New York, if for nothing else, the ease of going out and being able to eat whatever we want in a restaurant. Such is also the case in Israel.

Both our girls studied there this past summer. Kelly and I traveled with Rabbi Zaklos to see them and do some touring. So everything was good about this trip, like all those things I mentioned above. The one thing that I had so much difficulty with was how many people came up to me asking or begging for money. It happened all the time at the Kotel, and I think at every synagogue where the rabbi and I prayed, and we went to quite a few. They were of all ages, from elderly to boys in their teens. Some were dressed pretty darn well. Was I supposed to give them all something? Should I have been making a judgment as to who needed more? So I struggled with that for the better part of a week.

When we went to Tzfat, one of the things Rabbi Zaklos wanted to do was take a dip in the Arizal's mikveh. Rabbi Isaac Luria, who lived in the sixteenth century, is widely regarded as one the preeminent Kabbalists of all time. This mikveh, which he went to daily, is notable for being quite cold and only reachable by walking down hundreds of steps. I was game for this. The plan was to go there and then meet my wife and Carolyn for lunch. Since we were going to walk from the hotel where we were staying, and I was going to take my clothes off in the mikveh, it didn't make a lot of sense to take my wallet with me. So I took it out of my back pocket and put it on the back seat of the rental car and covered it with some clothes. Off the two of us went, down the million stairs (it's getting longer), and into the mikveh. It was nice and cold. Actually, that was not a bad thing, since it was over ninety-five degrees that day. So then it was all the way back up the bazillion stairs to the car. We drove a short distance, parked, and as I was walking away, I realized I needed my wallet. So I turned around but it wasn't in the back seat. I looked in the car, under the car, then over and over again. We drove back to the hotel parking lot and looked around. None of this made any sense. The car doors had been locked. I was so sure that I had taken my wallet out and put it in the car. Rabbi Zaklos asked if I wanted to walk back down to the mikveh to see if it was there. Frankly, I would rather tovil a refrigerator. Really, though, even if I had had it in my back pocket there, he had been next to my clothes when I went into the mikveh.

That was miserable and frustrating. Besides the credit cards, there was $300 in cash. It took me half a day to get over feeling upset and to deal with the credit cards. Something else, though, helped put it in perspective. Kelly had gone clothes shopping and had told the story of my wallet to the shopkeeper. Apparently, without hesitation, she told my wife that Hashem must have taken it. When Kelly related this to me, it all made sense. That was how God helped me resolve my tzedakah dilemma.

The Covenant

Being Jewish is no easy trick. Being The Chosen People, picked by God from among all the nations, certainly has its benefits, but there are obligations too. I have certainly had my share of struggles in the course of becoming more observant. But I am pleased to report that each one has brought with it a sense of satisfaction and a benefit to both myself and those around me.

So I was studying with Rabbi Zaklos and Kelly. We were reviewing holidays and lifecycle events. We were talking about the bris, and he was explaining some of the halachot. He was going into great detail as to everything that is required. A thought came to me, and it wasn't the most pleasant thought— what if my bris had not been done in a completely "kosher" manner? I was not liking the answer I was coming up with as he was detailing all the specifics required. It seemed like an entirely reasonable question to ask Rabbi Zaklos. It also seemed like an entirely reasonable question to take to my grave.

The conversation went on just a tad longer before I couldn't stand it anymore. So I asked. Oops. I shouldn't have asked.

The issue at hand centered on who performed my bris. Was it an Orthodox rabbi or not? It seemed pretty straightforward at this point that I needed to ask my mom. I did, and she informed me it was a local pediatrician. Oy.

The next step (after a modicum of procrastination) was to call Rabbi Gil Leeds, the Chabad Shaliach to the University of California, Berkeley, and an often-used mohel in Northern California. He was gracious, kind, and a fountain of information. The good news was that I did not have to have the whole thing done again. The bad news was that there was something that did need to be done. The object of the game was to now obtain a lancet (a tiny needle), and do the deed with the proper blessing. Oy vey.

So I went about trying to get a lancet. I went to the local CVS pharmacy where Erin, the pharmacist, has treated my patients and me kindly in the past. I asked her for a lancet. She asked, "Why do you need it?" I answered, "Can we just skip it?"

She handed me an open box, virtually full of lancets, and told me she didn't need them since it was an open box, and I could have them all. Swell. Just in case I don't get it right the first time, I could do it one hundred times more.

At this point I'd like to transfer you, dear reader, to the e-mail exchange I had with Rabbi Leeds. This sequence, which I've placed in chronological order, will take you through right to the end.

From: jfinemd@yahoo.com

Subject: Re: bris

To: giljleeds@hotmail.com

Hi Rabbi

Since I passed out during our conversation (kidding) I need a quick review.

What are the 3 things you mentioned to make a circumcision kosher?

And, I think I do get it, but can I do it in the wrong place...or ultimately, a drop and the blessing is sufficient?

Thanks for your ongoing help

Joel

From: Rabbi Gil Y. Leeds <giljleeds@hotmail.com>

To: jfinemd@yahoo.com

Subject: RE: bris

Hi Dr. Fine,

Sorry for not getting back to you sooner —it's been a crazy day.

Just to summarize—the bris can be subdivided into 3 parts a) being circumcised b) not being uncircumcised c) the act of the bris.

You have 2 out of 3 parts already (a and b) and now by doing the "hatafa" (i.e. drop of blood), you are doing the act of the bris in a 100% kosher manner. You need to draw a speck of blood with a lancet from the 12 o'clock position on the band of skin located behind the ridge of the glans and before you do that (while you're still modestly covered), you should say "L'Shaim Mitzvas Hatafas Dam Bris Kodesh" and then you are done.

Feel free to call or write with any more questions or updates…

All the best and Shabbat shalom!

GIL

From: "Joel Fine, M.D." <jfinemd@yahoo.com>
To: Rabbi Gil Y. Leeds <giljleeds@hotmail.com>
Subject: Re: bris

Very helpful. I think I'm waiting till Sunday. Should I invite guests? Anyone want to be the standing sandek?

Good Shabbos to you and yours!

Joel

From: Rabbi Gil Y. Leeds <giljleeds@hotmail.com>
To: jfinemd@yahoo.com
Subject: RE: bris

☺

From: jfinemd@yahoo.com
Subject: Re: bris
To: giljleeds@hotmail.com

simon tov oo mazel tov, simon tov u mazel tov, simon tov oo mazel tov, aa aa lanooo oo…

Thanks for your help

From: giljleeds@hotmail.com

To: jfinemd@yahoo.com

Subject: RE: bris

mazel tov! mazel tov!

Hope it was not too bad…

I of course also had to tell Rabbi Zaklos of the momentous event. I believe I sent him the e-mail exchanges as well, but also added that with all the extra lancets I had, we could do the entire community together.

3

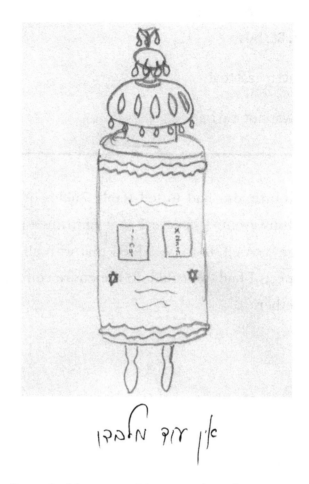

אל יוון אלחנן

It probably goes without saying that my path was not entirely independent of what was going on in my family. Carolyn was valedictorian of her high school class and earned the chance to give a speech at graduation. The graduation ceremony was set to take place in the football stadium on Shavuos, the holiday commemorating the giving of the Ten Commandments. This holiday is similar to a Shabbos where there is no work, driving, use of electricity, etc., but on a holiday you are able to carry things away from the home, something that you cannot do on Shabbos. Being the upwardly mobile Jewish family that we were, we would stay at a nearby hotel and walk to graduation, not a big deal. But the electricity thing was shaping up to be a problem. What about her use of a microphone when she gave her speech? This was not easy for us. I really wanted to hear my kid give a speech. I know she wanted to give it too. It might have been a little more difficult for Carolyn, since her sister gave a great valedictory address a couple years before. I saw her struggling, and I certainly wanted to fix the problem for her. Although my wife had a clear understanding of the Jewish law of the situation, I had to ask my LOR (local Orthodox rabbi) anyway to see if there was any wiggle room. It turned out that since the graduation was going to be held in the evening, there was a slight possibility that nightfall (the end of the holiday) would occur before she was scheduled to give her speech. Unfortunately, upon checking into that with the school, we discovered that it would simply not be the case. Maybe she could talk really loud or just deliver this speech to the few people that would be able to hear her. I struggled with this. I wanted to provide guidance and good counsel and found myself quite torn.

Between the ages of ten and eighteen, I probably shot more baskets than Michael Jordan did. I spent countless hours on the driveway by myself, just shooting. I got pretty good at it. After high school I developed into a pretty decent player. I almost made the JV team at UCLA as a walk-on. That was okay, because I got to play plenty of good basketball in intramural leagues there and in a variety of other leagues until I needed a hip replacement at age forty. My defense, ability to move without the ball, and passing were okay, not great, but I knew how to score.

One of the guys I went up against a lot in local games in Vacaville was a guy named Smitty. He was a really good all-around player who played for the local junior college. He would take it upon himself to guard me when we were on opposite teams, and he played aggressively. It would not be unusual that he would hack me up. One day I came home with a few more gashes than usual. Samantha was four or five at the time. She asked what happened, and I explained that Smitty had done that to me. I still get a kick out of it to this day when I think of what happened a few weeks later. I came in from working in the yard, and I had gotten scratched up from dealing with the rosebushes. Samantha looked at me and asked, "Did Smitty do that to you?"

Here's why I told you that story. I was once on Smitty's team, and he took a pass and immediately threw an elegant, simple bounce pass to a teammate who was open under the basket for an easy bucket. I asked right away, "How come I can't do that?" And he answered right away, "Because you look to shoot first." Maybe you had to be there, but his comment came across as profound and wise.

So I told you that story to now tell you this one. There was an adult men's recreation softball league game where I grounded out to end the game. I lamented to my good friend, teammate, and colleague

Tom Batter that I had cost us the game. Tom, who had played catcher in college for the University of California, Berkeley, scolded me quickly and thoroughly. "It was a seven-inning game, and there were three outs each inning. Why would you think that your out at the end of the game was any more significant than the other twenty? Somebody else could have stretched a double into a triple, or made a fielding play that they didn't." Basically Tom was explaining to me what a team sport was. My athletic development consisted primarily of shooting baskets by myself. I was, and probably still am, at risk of taking on too much responsibility in a team situation.

Parenting is ideally a two-person job. And, in fact, life itself is a team sport. Both can be done by one person. I've seen this happen personally and professionally, and it's way harder. Generally speaking, the results aren't as good. It's not an accident that it is set up the way that it is. In a family there is the mom and dad, both bringing separate skill sets to the game.

What Kelly and I did in this situation, for better or worse, was to leave the decision up to Carolyn. So, essentially, it was not for me or us to decide. We said we were both okay if she decided to give her speech. That would certainly be the easier thing to do. She decided the thing to do was to not give her speech. The administration at Vacaville High School was supportive of her decision and worked with her to come up with the plan of prerecording her speech, so she could remain fully observant of the holiday.

Suffice it to say, the wife and I were very proud of the kid, and I certainly appreciate all the positive attention she got for her decision, all well-deserved. Here again, besides being a role model for her dad and Jews everywhere, I'm reminded of how efficient team play can be. I didn't have to make the decision, nor did Kelly. Our teammate did, and she handled it just fine. The level of observance for all of Team Fine went up that day. And because it was written up in the local paper and mentioned in a segment on the Channel 13 news, her play could have far more reaching effects.

In fact, a few months later, a thirteen-year-old wrote an article in a national girls' Jewish magazine about how Carolyn was a role model for her. We also know that Carolyn received acknowledgment and compliments from people in New York and as far away as Israel. Her actions were roundly regarded as a kiddush Hashem. A dear friend told me the event was bigger than Sinai. There is, of course, at least a similarity, since there were no microphones used there either.

Carolyn set the bar higher, and I tacitly agreed to the new standard. I do not recall any specific changes I made, but I was now more apt to make decisions commensurate with a higher level of observance. What is it that leads someone to increase his or her level of observance? Why do we change our behaviors? The bottom-line answer is pretty straightforward: It's too complicated to explain. On top of the bottom line, however, I can share some ideas and thoughts that lend to an understanding of the process that is all around us, yet difficult to understand.

I tell patients that 70 percent of changing a behavior is developing the insight and understanding of why we do what we do; 30 percent is then practicing the new behavior. My job is to facilitate the discovery process, and then teach ways to manage situations differently. One of my patients benefited significantly from recognizing that his interactions with his boss were reminiscent of how he interacted with his father when younger. Approaching the boss with this in mind made a huge difference, and the feedback I received was that it was much easier to change because of the new, deeper understanding of this early relationship. However, we don't always know the influences that lead to someone's actions. A patient might present to me with an addiction to a substance or a set of behaviors. Twelve-step programs are remarkably productive vehicles that can facilitate change without much attention being paid to the underlying cause of the addictive behavior. A common denominator to individual therapy and a twelve step program is the importance of a relationship with a mentor—someone who can be respected, knows the ropes, and can demonstrate the right behavior. In twelve-step programs that is the role of the sponsor. In the therapy example, that would be my job. You can wonder, since there is not a shortage of role models in the world, nor parents, for that matter. Why is it so hard to change?

As I mentioned before, we are resistant to change. We find comfort in leaving things just as they are, good and bad. This omnipresent impediment to change is compounded by the fact that essentially all of us have an inflated sense of being able to predict the future.

I hear all the time in resistance to trying something different, "Well, if I do that, then this will happen." No, actually, we have no clue. I've noticed from a recent perusal of the sports pages that NFL placekickers are now making over 99 percent of their extra-point attempts. In fact, at this point of the 2012 season, near the halfway point, the top eight kickers in each league are yet to miss. But if you think about it, the next time your team jogs out onto the field for an extra point attempt, you have no idea if it will be blocked or if the kick will be shanked to the side.

I've given some patients a challenge; those who take me up on it have always been surprised. Get a small notebook and start writing down your predictions about what a family member will say or do in a particular situation. Maybe it will be the reaction of a spouse when you get home on a given day in a particular situation, or what the kids will do if you tell them to do something. What you'll find is that you're absolutely horrible at predicting what's going to happen. What we remember are the times that we were right. We conveniently forget the times we were wrong. As Art Zafiropoulo, CEO of Ultratech, is fond of saying, "All forecasts are wrong; that's why there are revised forecasts."

With due respect to our differing tolerances for risk, how much change takes place will be correlated with how well we know, trust, and value the relationship with the model. I have described change that can be imperceptible and gradual, or it can be rapid and bone-crushing. Ultimately we drive our own vehicle of change, and we control the pedals for the gas and brakes. Who is in the car with us has a lot to do with where we go and how long the trip takes.

4

One of my patients whom I had known for several years once paid me a very nice compliment. She had been studying Judaism on her own and told me one reason why she became interested in Judaism was because of the way I walked the walk and talked the talk. My Yiddishkeit has certainly affected my practice over the years, which in turn has affected my patients. I don't wear a yarmulke in the office and my tzitzit are tucked in. It would not be a mystery, however, to the casual observer in my office that I am Jewish. The metaphors and stories I use to make a point often contain a biblical reference, political comment, or stereotypic manner that frequently has me labeled Jewish (and also, for whatever it's worth, as hailing from New York). One out of two isn't bad.

The only time I can remember my religion clearly working against me, or my patient, was an Afghan woman who seemed to appreciate and benefit from our first visit. Right before we ended, she noticed hanging on the wall a framed version of the Prayer of Maimonides for the physician. She asked about it, and then the tone in the room changed. I had already given her an appointment for a follow-up visit that she had seemed interested in keeping. However, shortly after that first visit, she canceled our next appointment and did not return my call that was intended to inquire as to what had changed.

Save for that incident, it seems to be in everybody's best interests that Judaica flows freely here. In fact, many years ago, I offered members of a group therapy some Yiddish refrigerator magnets that were lying around and not being put to use by me. One of my patients was quite pleased to take me up on the offer. Then, last year some time, my coffee cup went missing. I turned the office upside down and asked everybody where the heck it was. It was beyond me how someone could have walked out of my office with a coffee cup that had "Dr. Fine" written on it in big letters. But it turns out that's what happened. One of my patients named Carmen (her real name) told me she heard from her sister Becky that her husband, who was in another group therapy in the office, had used my cup and walked out with it. I couldn't believe it! Why in the world would he walk out of the office with my coffee cup? I played it up a bit for entertainment value. Carmen told me she would pass on my concerns to her sister.

As it turns out, Becky (her real name) was the one who had taken advantage of the free Yiddish magnets offer. Soon after I had seen Carmen, my cup was returned with the following note:

Shalom Dr. Fine,

Remember that box of Yiddish magnets you gave me long ago? Well here is my attempt to put them to use.

Here is your coffee cup that my gonif of a husband took without permission. He has got some chutzpah!! Had I known you became so verklempt when you discovered it was missing I would have returned it sooner. I did not realize how important it is to you. I truly thought it was just a drek or schlocky souvenir.

I am glad that the cup is back safe and sound in your hands and I no longer have to dayge that it will get broken in my home. It was causing me great kvetch.

Sincerely,

The goy gal—Rebecca

PS—I hope you are laughing now as much as I was when I wrote this!

Yes, Becky, I was.

I have noticed how my level of observance has changed my approach to patients. It's been for several years now that I feel an obligation to let couples who seek therapy know that I have a bias to work with them to save their marriage. When I was first in practice, this was not the case. There were situations where I might have introduced the treatment plan or reflected on a couple's progress and indicated that a successful therapy might still end in divorce.

It is also not unusual for me to introduce Shabbat observance as part of a treatment plan—certainly not in a literal sense, since there is not an obligation on the non-Jew to observe the Sabbath. However, I have found in clinical practice that for some patients carving out a set period of time on a specific day and remembering it and guarding it can be very helpful for a variety of conditions. Let me expound on this.

I mentioned before that Shabbat in my childhood home was marked by candle lighting and special dishes. This level of observance did not continue when I moved away from home. The rituals and blessings were rekindled after Kelly and I were married. Shabbat day, however, was not unique until we were hanging out with Rabbi Kopstein. Recall that I was doing yard work (which I had asked about), so except for the time spent in the synagogue, it was just another day. As we became more observant with Chabad in Pleasanton, we were learning the exact rules regarding what you can and can't do. We very much enjoyed Shabbat services on Saturday, as well as being part of the small community in Pleasanton, but complete Shabbos observance still seemed undoable. Still, going every week facilitated our progress with the prayer service, allowed us to have our questions asked and answered, and simultaneously we observed some wonderful role models in the Resnicks.

It didn't happen for a while, but the time eventually came when we decided as a family to stop driving and assume responsibility for not doing work of any kind, consistent with the Halacha. Our progress has been gradual. It is mindboggling and I dare say impossible to take on all the Shabbos mitzvos at once. "Steady as she goes" has done the trick for us.

Since we have become Shabbat observant, my weekends are profoundly different. It's hard to completely understand how this works, but when I return to the office on Monday, it invariably feels like I've been away for a long time. I can remember when we were not Shabbat observant, and I would go back to the office after doing yard work, watching some football on TV, hanging out with the family, and doing whatever...it would not be unusual for it to feel like I had just left the office. So now I leave work on Friday, prepare for the Sabbath, and then observe the holiday. It is a day of complete rest. There is no use of electricity, no TV, no radio, and no driving anywhere. It's not unusual that I will walk to Rabbi Zaklos's home, 4.6 miles from where I live. Once a month, we have a planned larger community gathering at his home. Kelly and I will stay at a hotel on Shabbos night and walk the short distance to his house. Sunday is my day for doing yard work and puttering around the house. It is hard to believe that I still get everything done I need to get done, and I go back to work feeling like I just took a vacation.

So I try and communicate some of these advantages in a modified form to a variety of patients whose conditions sound they like they could use a break. Many patients have taken me up on the suggestion by setting aside three hours where they are Shabbat-observant in some kind of way. The feedback is invariably positive. This treatment recommendation usually comes with a short dissertation on the fourth commandment where we learn, as I indicated above, that the Sabbath must be remembered in order for it to happen, but just as importantly, it has to be guarded. If you don't remember it, it won't happen…but you also have to protect and guard the time, and not let anything, under any circumstance, supersede the time of this break.

It turns out the fifth commandment comes up all the time in treatment as well. Many people who come to see me have issues with their parents because of how they experience the way their parents have acted toward them. Helping patients understand this relationship in the context of their obligation to honor their parents—and to understand what that means—is invariably helpful. To honor your parents is to be the best doggone person you can be, a real mensch. Respecting your parents is a subset of honoring them. By providing for their basic needs (if necessary) and demonstrating a reverence to them, you not only are showing respect, but also honoring them, since these acts of respect are part of what makes up a very special person. Notice please that the above actions can be carried out, irrespective of how your parents have behaved or acted themselves.

In fact, understanding all the Ten Commandments as a whole for what they are—utterances spoken by

God to the Israelites at Mount Sinai—serves as a counterbalance to a common problem that comes up all the time. I'm not a fan of when I hear my patients talking about how they *should* do this or they *should* do that. I explain that substituting the word *should* with *could* is invariably anxiolytic—it reduces stress. "I *could* take out the trash before dinner" portends less angst than "I *should* take out the trash before dinner." The exception, I go on to say, would be the Ten Commandments. You really *should* do those. It helps to understand that we have obligations that should not be transgressed, but the choices we make in most all of our life activities are indeed choices: we *could* do this, or we *could* do that.

So dear reader, allow me to ride this tangent off into the distance. We will return later to interesting patient anecdotes.

Uncertainty in our choices, compounded by the juxtaposition of *could* and *should*, invariably leads us to experience ambivalence. Ambivalence is a special kind of uncertainty where you might flip-flop back and forth, possibly not even aware of your uncertainty, but experiencing stress and anxiety. Mental health is our ability to deal with ambivalence. We have different types of defenses and coping mechanisms that result in different styles, character traits, and behaviors to deal with ambivalence. It's usually the case that gathering knowledge is an integral part of resolving our aforementioned ambivalence. If I didn't know whether I should buy a Honda or Toyota, and flip-flopped between them, you could say I was ambivalent. Acquiring knowledge (in this case, facts about the cars), including learned and informed opinions from others, moves me to the preferred position where I am like an expert on the subject at hand. From that standpoint there is less likely to be buyer's remorse after the decision is made. I further ease my psychological burden by keeping track of the difference between *should* and *could.* Allowing myself the freedom and flexibility to make a choice, coupled with having acquired knowledge about the matter at hand, puts me in a position to more gracefully choose the car that is best for me.

I have had my share of ambivalence myself, and it's my ongoing hope and practice that I will resolve my cosmic dilemmas as they appear. A real good one happened a couple years ago when I was meeting with an adolescent named John. He came to see me because he was having bad dreams. I took a history, made a nice connection with him, and gave him brilliant advice and counsel on how he could manage his symptoms. We were wrapping things up, and I asked if he had any questions for me. And he did. He asked if I was Jewish. I said sure and wondered out loud what made him bring that up. He said that his dad and stepmom had been driving recently and had seen me "walking from church" with my yarmulke on. I asked what struck him about that, and he told me that his mom was Jewish.

Oh boy...bells were now ringing in my head...blue light special...ding ding ding. He didn't know that he was Jewish (!) I didn't know what to do with this. I stalled and asked if his mom's mom was Jewish. He said yes. I remained ambivalent, but I was gathering knowledge.

So I was supposed to say something now, because this has to do with his soul. Is there anything more important than that? Yeah, what about the fact that he came to see me for bad dreams, and I just did a good job of taking care of that problem? What I needed to do was shake his hand and say good-bye.

Well, that's not what I did.

"Did you know that that makes you Jewish?"

His eyes got as big as saucers.

I explained matrilineal descent and my willingness to see him again down the line if he had any more problems with the dreams, or even questions about this Jewish stuff. He was appreciative, and he told me he hoped that his mom would go to Jewish church and take him. The last thing we did was talk about a good firm handshake. I have taken it upon myself to cure the world of weak handshakes.

So the session was over, but my head was spinning. Did I just do good, or did I just go where no man (psychiatrist) has gone before—or at least shouldn't? I needed to collect more information. I looked forward to my Tuesday consultation group.

Since I've been in practice, I have had a weekly Tuesday group supervision with other psychiatrists and therapists in my office. I think this type of clinical experience is invaluable, and for all intents and purposes, mandatory to do what we do for a living. My group has provided the opportunity for each of us to talk about cases or about our own difficulties, struggles, and questions as mental health practitioners.

So the next Tuesday, I ran it up the flagpole. It was not saluted. Essentially shots were fired. My colleagues explained that I'm the doctor, not the rabbi. Some argued with my definition of who is Jewish, saying that was my opinion and not necessarily true. With four others in the room—two of them Jewish themselves—it seemed the universal opinion was that I went over the line.

Yeah, yeah, yeah...I get what they were saying. I don't know, though; I might play that hand exactly the same way if it comes up again. There is no question that this was not what he came to see me for...or was it? A high percentage of folk like you and me believe that life has a purpose, that there is a God that runs the world, and thus, nothing happens by accident.

So here's a Jewish kid, out in Vacaville, who just got introduced to the fact that he has a Jewish soul. We'll see what happens next.

5

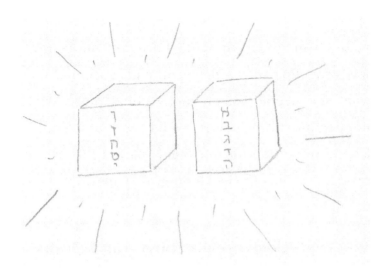

One of the things I love about my job, which is commensurate with my increased level of observance, is how much Torah study plays into improving one's life. Certainly it has for me, and it's my sincere hope my patients benefit as well.

I think I've established in my own brain that I'm not a rabbi, but part of what I do is teach. How I teach is based on my own experience and a sense of what would be most helpful to the patient. A good rule to follow as a therapist is you should very carefully screen any personal experience story about yourself. Before I say *I*, I want to make sure that it's in the best interests of the patient.

So Carmen (yes, the same Carmen from before) was struggling with a problem, and it seemed that what she needed was a motivational push. What popped into my head was to tell her about the drash I had just written for our family blog. I thought to myself, you've got to be kidding; are you really going to tell her that?

At the beginning of this Jewish year, Kelly came up with an idea for a family blog. We would each post a picture and a drash, or a commentary based on that week's Torah portion. I think it has been a really cool idea, and some of the stuff we've come up with is really great. So I happened to be particularly proud of the piece I had done that week. I had included a picture of a Nike swoosh with the title, "Just Do It!"

This was completely apropos to Carmen's issues, but, oh my goodness, did she really need all this? I weighed out the pros and cons—things like how much of my drive to share this was due to my own excitement about the project versus the value of leaving my stuff out of the discourse, since it would just be a distraction to helping Carmen. Well, since I recognize that my enthusiasm and energy is part of what can drive a point home, I geared up and let it rip, paraphrasing the following:

In the Torah portion for this week titled Tzav, meaning command, there is the fourth and final shalshelet, which is a cantillation mark that indicates a musical sequence. A generally accepted way to understand this particular cantillation mark is that it highlights a word indicating uncertainty, a difficult decision, or mixed feelings. The first shashelet in the Torah is found on a word meaning that Lot was delaying. The second is when Abraham's servant Eliezer was hesitating with the profound responsibility of finding and bringing back a wife for Isaac. The third is when Joseph refused the advances of Potiphor's wife. But here in our portion, the shashelet appears on the word "vayishchat," which means essentially "and it was slaughtered." This was done by Moses, completely in keeping with the command of

God. It is very difficult to understand how this fits the standard shashelet pattern.

One classic understanding is that Moses wanted to have Aaron's position, but was uneasy about that. If this were the case, it would fit more in line with the other shashelets. I found that to be a bit of a stretch, though, and wondered if there was a better way to see it.

If we take a step back, we see that Moses slaughtered this particular ram and a second ram for the purposes of ordination. He took some of its blood and put it on Aaron's ear, hand, and toe. He did the same thing to Aaron's sons and then continued on with his sacrificial responsibilities.

Consider that this takes place after Moses had spent face time with God. One of the ways that Moses is special and remarkable is that he heard what his own future held. He was given the entire Torah by God. Since that was the case, he knew that Aaron's sons would take things a bit too far at one point and were destined to be consumed by fire. I anticipate here is where we find Moses in full hesitation mode. He knows what is going to happen to Aaron's sons because of their own actions, yet he is about to ordain them as high priests.

We can appreciate from this angle the continuity of the traditional understanding for our shashelet. We can also learn from Moses's actions here that he was the number-one practitioner when it comes to naasaeh vinishma: "we will first do what God tells us, then we will listen." Although there was a hesitation, he knew that it was time to "Just Do It," because that's what the commandment, the Tzav, is for today.

I checked with her the following week, and she reported our discussion had been very helpful. She not only appreciated the content, which was the encouragement to push forward, but also the process—the way I delivered it—gave her a deeper understanding of what she needed to do. I think that is just so cool.

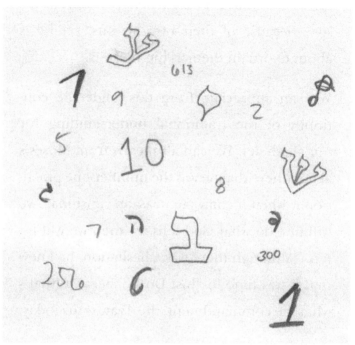

Many of my weekly blog postings have examples of gematria. This is quite a contrast to where I was at Mosaic Law. Remember, at that time, I thought gematria was contrived and artificial. My perspective is certainly different now. It follows for me that if the Torah is the word of God, it's not conceivable there are superfluous words or letters. I think this is consistent with the intricacies we easily see within our own bodies, climates, the food chain, and all of nature. Given the fact that every Hebrew letter is also a number, it strikes me as apparent there can be relationships between words, sentences, and even entire portions discerned from their numerical value. In my current armamentarium, I have a dictionary of all the words in the Bible in order of their numerical value and a new app for my iPhone that quickly calculates numerical values and related words and sentences.

What I've come up with so far pales in comparison to discovering the atom or even making a kosher Pop-Tart, but there are lessons that can be reinforced, and I love to explore these mathematical vistas. I am convinced there is gold to be discovered by continuing to dig.

Something I found a few months ago in the portion Va'eschanan in Deuteronomy, where it was explained that God would dislodge seven nations in order for the promised land to be delivered to the Israelites, was that by using a gematria principle, which allows the total number of words in a phrase to be added to the actual numerical value itself, the words "...before you the Hittites, Girgashites,

Amorites, Cannanites, Perizzites, Hivites and Jebusites" interestingly have the same numerical value as Syria, Iran, Iraq, Jordan, Egypt, Lebanon, and Turkey.[*]

Some of my blog postings have had a lighter flair. With this particular one there was a picture of our daughters on the airport tram waving good-bye as they headed off to New York. With it, I posted the following:

> Near the end of our parsha, Yosef is overcome with emotion at the sight of his younger blood brother, Binyamin. He excuses himself from the room to weep, returns, and favors his younger brother by giving him five times the portion of the others. When they leave he has his silver goblet placed in Binyamin's bag, apparently as part of a ploy to have him return.
>
> Is there more to the ploy? Do cats have fur? It is relevant to note that the word for goblet

---

The principle of im hateivos means the gematria of מפניך החתי והגרגשי והאמרי והכנעני והפרזי והחוי והיבוסי is 2073, which is equal to סוריה ואיראן ועיראק וירדן ומצרים ולבנון וטורקיה using im hakollel.

גביע means trophy in Modern Hebrew. Yosef gave Binyamin something very special. There is a deeper meaning found in the gematria of the specific goblet, a silver one, גביע הכסף. The principle of im hateivos allows a figure of 252, which is the same as לברך "to bless." Yosef has further demonstrated his love and connection for his brother by the significance of the gift and the blessing.

In our family, we further this tradition by placing something in the suitcase of those who travel, for their merit, safety, and eventual return.

So what about you? If you are like 99-plus percent of the Jews in the world, you are not a tzadik, and thus have a little room to improve yourself. Let me try and sell you something. First, though, consider you don't always have to pay upfront, as we know very well from our mortgages, the plastic we carry, and the federal deficits we hear about. Next, I want to tell you that what I'm selling is a concept for your health and well-being for yourself and those around you. You don't have to pay me. It would be swell if you paid cash for the book, but whatever the case, the chances are also more than 99 percent, based on my clinical experience, that your well-being is integrally related to the sanctity of your relationships. So what I want you to buy into is the improved health and well-being that comes from an improved relationship with God.

Consider that trust is like psychological debt. It's a debt that can also be leveraged to increase the chances of bigger returns. I'll come back to this concept in a few moments. Our self-esteem, which is commonly understood to be a function of how we feel about ourselves and how confident we are, is really best thought of as a reservoir. When my self-esteem is good, meaning my reservoir is full, it will be easier to take criticism, insult, or other psychological damage and bounce right back, since I have reserves to draw from. Plus, you will just feel better. For instance, if someone expresses dissatisfaction and says something to you like "You're an idiot," if your reservoir is near full, it will be much easier to see such a comment as a function of his or her disappointment and not about you. On the other hand, if your reservoir is low, such a comment is much more likely to be taken personally, whether or not your behavior warranted the criticism.

How does this reservoir get formed and tanked up? It pretty much starts from birth and is a function of the empathic connections we received from our parents. When I say empathy, I'm referring to an active process where someone conveys to another that he or she knows what it is like to be the other person. That doesn't mean you have to feel what the other person feels. It means you have to understand the other person enough to be able to use facial expression, body language, or intonation of voice to communicate that you get what it's like to be him or her. The definition I just laid out is the science; the actual process of conveying empathy is an art.

If you were born into a family where your parents were good at this, you reaped significant rewards. When mom was holding you as a little baby, and you had a tummy ache and started to whine, did she look down at you with a concerned expression, conveying how sad this was, or did she send the message that she was frustrated because of the crying? In the first scenario, she was resonating with you. She may or may not have felt sad herself, but she was conveying that she got what it was like to be you. In the second example, it's about her.

Trouble is, with the second scenario, you are not getting feedback that what you actually feel is legit. You feel yucky, but your mirror is showing anger and frustration. This type of interaction happens a zillion times, certainly more times than there are steps down to the Arizal's mikveh. It's such an innocent parenting mistake to say, "You are making me angry." This has nothing to do with the kid's behavior being right or wrong and communicates the message that the child is responsible for the parent's feelings. It is better to convey you get where the child is coming from and, if anything, that your reaction to his behavior is your deal, not his. Please don't confuse this with setting limits and structure. Kids need rules and regulations absolutely for sure, big time and in spades. But sending the message of being responsible for the parent's feelings is not such a good idea. Being respectful, which is taught, and also empathic, which is demonstrated, is a great combo. Showing your kids how this is done is fabulous. Hence, the goals for parenting are threefold: to provide rules and structure, to be empathic, and to be a role model. Especially when the parents are firing on all three cylinders, the child will develop a sense of safety, comfort, and confidence. The empathic connections received and experienced are portending a healthy sense of self.

This is the process that takes place primarily in childhood and all throughout our lives: to make and then fill up that reservoir. There is a "vicious cycle" here that can go in a good direction. The more someone gets you and really understands you, the more likely you will want to be close to that person, and this builds confidence in the relationship. This feeds back into your own sense of yourself. If everybody around you seems to resonate with you, then you feel better about yourself. Notice, please, this does not mean if you are around someone who is depressed, and you are cheery and encouraging, he or she will feel better. In fact, it's probably most helpful if you convey to the person who is depressed that you get what it's like to be him or her. If you don't get the depressed person, or you can't understand why he or she is feeling like that, it's best then to leave the advice to the pros.

Remember, though, it's not just empathy we want from our relationships. We need structure and limits, ideally coming from a role model. So what do we do when we lack someone who fits this bill in our relationships? Well, if you're a kid, you are kind of out of luck. We're dependent by nature, and it takes a bunch of years until we can be out on our own and pick and choose relationships that will provide us what we missed. If you are an adult, you can come see me professionally, or reacquaint yourself with our creator.

It is clear that God provides us with rules and structure. In fact, most of them are conveniently written down in book form (Torah), and I'm sure there's an app for that. For me, the more I understand about the manual that came with the book (Talmud) and learn with the experts (rabbis) who understand it and practice its teachings, the more it is intuitively obvious that it's true.

I have also found it works for me psychologically to have God as a role model. Something I struggle with (but not as much as I used to) is how difficult it is to be satisfied with something I have done. It always seems like I could have done better. Then why in the world would I want God to be my role model? If I'm a perfectionist, or at least someone who's not satisfied unless it's perfect, which can't be done, why would I want to consciously hold myself to an infinitely high standard? Well, it's because of the other thing that God provides us: unconditional empathy. God gets us. He created us, sustains us, and is available to us 24/7. Along those lines, the greatest gift our creator bestowed upon us, besides existence itself, is the concept of teshuvah. To be able to return through repentance to God or our fellow human beings facilitates receiving the empathy integral to our well-being. Again, a vicious cycle, but in a good direction.

Now back to the aforementioned issue. Taking on any debt is a risk. We take a chance when we trust someone. For most of us, our faith in God can waver, making trust problematic. Let me sell you on the idea that taking the risk of trusting God carries with it a benefit-to-risk ratio that is extraordinarily high. To work at deepening your trust by studying and doing mitzvoth, you carry very little risk and the potential for essentially infinite reward. I can't think of any Jew I have ever met who would disagree with this last statement. Accelerate the level of intimacy you have with God, whether you are at a standstill or moving at a nice clip.

I have found that my sense of God's connectedness to me has been proportional to my level of observance. Our sages have taught that our souls are improved by the thoughts, speech, and actions that bring us closer to God. I have seen clinically my patients improve emotionally, behaviorally, and cognitively when they step up their religious observance. And I've experienced an improved quality of life commensurate with my sense of connectedness to our creator.

7

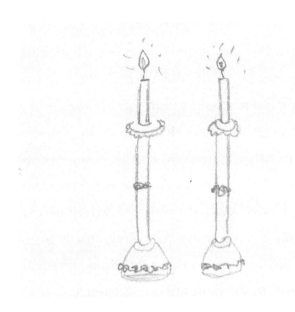

I am clearly more observant than I used to be. I take some pride in that, and it sure seems that my wife and daughters appreciate the strides I have made. My rabbis seem pleased with my progress, and it's not much of a leap to assume that friends and colleagues in the community are as well. Although it's not as easy to measure, the entire world Jewish community benefits from one of its own becoming more observant. How can this be anything other than what our creator wants from us? My ongoing challenge, which I anticipate is shared by anyone who reads this, is to plug away and improve my Yiddishkeit. Everybody benefits.

Do I do all of the mitzvoth? Pray with sincere dedication and focus all the time? Nah. But I've done so much and come so far! And it's obvious I have so far to go! But isn't that a metaphor for discerning our purpose here on earth? The more we learn, whether it is in the study of science where we call it the universe or in our religion where we call it God, infinite is the word. And slow, steady progress is the way to unravel the mysterious, mystical, and unknown to substantiate our existence.

That brings us up to just a few months ago. It was Passover, and we went to a KMR organized retreat. No cleaning up the house, getting rid of the chametz, bringing in all new stuff, dishes, food. We just packed up and drove to Southern California. Everything was taken care of. The Jews took over the Park Hyatt Aviara Resort. There were about eight hundred of us. The food was absolutely incredible. It was like a cruise on land. There was great entertainment; the speakers were wonderful. It was on the second to the last night, Shabbos, when we went to a panel discussion on the spectrum of Orthodox Judaism. It was a late-night event, scheduled to start at 10:30, I guess Jewish time. There were only about a dozen people in the audience at several minutes after the scheduled starting time, with just two of the rabbis up on the panel. Rabbi Avrohom Lieberman said rhetorically, "We could begin if we had a moderator." Since my wife was not in the room, and she is the one who is responsible for keeping me in line, I got up and went to the front of the room and started to moderate. Rabbi Lieberman was clearly game, and things were going along fine. In fact, I heard someone mumble in the audience, "Hey, this guy is good." So that went on for ten minutes or so, until the real moderator came. Before I went back to my seat, Rabbi Lieberman walked over and asked me what my story was. I gave him the short version of what you've just read. He said to me, "You should write a book." I appreciated the indirect compliment. I lamented that Rabbi Zaklos had encouraged me as well, but I hadn't figured out how to get the thing going. I shared that Samantha had suggested I first focus on the question of who my target audience would be. Right away he told me, "For unaffiliated

Jews." His words were like a bonk on the head, but a good one. What a great idea. He told me he would be glad to review a draft. I assured him that I would take him up on the offer.

Rabbi Zaklos and his family don't go to the movie theaters. I can understand that, since it's primarily just junk anyway. In fact, we made the family decision several years ago to not have a television in our own home. I think we have benefited significantly from that decision, and looking at how busy we were, it's amazing to think that we ever had the time to watch as much as we did. So that said, there has been some stuff on the big and small screen of quality. One of my favorite movies of all time is *Field of Dreams*. I thought it would be fun to watch it with Rabbi Zaklos, so I talked him into an evening together. As many times as I've seen the film in the past, I never realized how many Jewish themes come out in the movie, such as the concepts of the messianic age, that the dead will return, and that heaven is as much here as it is above us. The importance of doing teshuva and how the righteous will be rewarded in the world to come are depicted in the movie very well.

I am particularly drawn to Burt Lancaster's character and the way he talks about being a doctor, essentially saying that it was his calling. I've thought for the longest time that I was born to be a shrink. I love everything about it. His character is a paradigm of virtue, as he shows not only his devotion to his work and to caring for his patients, but also his devotion to his family and the pursuit of extraneous pleasures. For him, it was baseball. Having fun and seeing life as an adventure is part of the way it's supposed to work. He resonated contentment at the end of his life. It helps to recognize that our ubiquitous quest for happiness is better framed by understanding it flows directly from contentment. Looking back, my life path has been headed toward the development of more Yiddishkeit. I have had wonderful role models, from my parents and rabbis to my wife and daughters. It's fulfilling and satisfying to know that I have a Jewish soul. This has meant a more spiritual connection with God, both literally and figuratively. Defining my life in terms of serving Hashem—whether it is in the care of others, being a role model myself, or performing mitzvoth—promotes an important sense of contentment.

Back to the Passover retreat. Another really cool thing was that the eight hundred observant Jews in attendance were made up of all kinds. There were Litvish Jews and Chassidic Jews. Everybody got along. Maybe it's because we were being fed really, really well. But the prayer services were led by different members of each community with their own traditions, and they all went along smoothly with an air of respect. Could anyone argue with this paradigm: Respect for your fellow Jew, ritual observance of a holiday within a community and following the track of your own arc, as it goes toward a better connection with God by following the commandments of our creator.

Epilogue

The Zakloses have done wonders since they came here just over three years ago. The Jewish community in Vacaville and Solano County has been unified under the auspices of an Orthodox rabbi and his wife. The Fines and the Kaplows are united again in a Jewish community that is becoming closer and more observant all time.

This is due to three components that also describe a parallel process to my own arc through Judaism. First, Chaim and Aidel Zaklos are both accessible. It has been very important for our community, as well as my own personal growth, that there is and has been a readily available teacher who provides information, support, and encouragement. They have not just been welcoming at the front door, but also once inside each time you come back. Secondly, these mentors have been role models. They show how it is done—how to talk the talk and walk the walk. It is much easier to want to emulate a leader when he or she not only conveys what needs to be done, but demonstrates it consistently. Finally, nothing in this universe happens without God's involvement. Our continued existence as a Jewish people, given the adversity we have faced, begs for the conclusion that there is a godly force ensuring our survival. It has become readily apparent to me, just as the Baal Shem Tov taught, that if a leaf falls off a tree and tumbles across the road, none of it happens without God's intervention. So it is with our community and my own level of observance, and everything else in our world, all of which is something to be eternally grateful for.

Acknowledgements

In addition to the good Lord, there are a variety of people who made choices and proved to be very supportive and helpful. First and foremost, of course, are my parents, Larry and Irene Fine. Good work, I daresay. My dear wife and bashert, Kelly, is a wonderful counterbalance to most of my meshugaas. My daughters, Samantha and Carolyn, are the best role models I have to be a wonderful human being. Sam also loaned her mad Pictionary drawing skills, and Care contributed her indefatigable ability to listen to me rant. My sister Sari showed me how to write a book, and my brother Gil showed me how to proofread one. My rabbis and teachers and friends, Kopstein, Resnick, and Zaklos, to whom I remain close and hope to continue to learn from for years to come. And my eternal gratefulness to a long list of friends, colleagues, and patients, who hang with me and form a team that I want to keep playing for indefinitely.

Glossary

Afikomen
: A broken piece of matzoh traditionally hid during the Passover seder to be found later, usually by the kids, and exchanged for prize.

Basketball
: The best sport ever.

Bimah
: The stage or pulpit in the synagogue.

Bris
: Literally "covenant of circumcision." Ritual circumcision performed on the eighth day for newborn Jewish boys.

Chabad
: One of the largest Chassidic movements in Judaism. Probably best known today in the Jewish and non-Jewish world for its outreach programs and efforts to increase the observance of Jews all over the world.

Chametz — Foods that are forbidden to be eaten on Passover. Usually contain leavening of some sort.

Crown Heights — Home of the world headquarters for Chabad, located in Brooklyn, New York.

Daven — To pray

Drash — Like a sermon. An exegesis of biblical text.

Halacha — Jewish law. Plural is halachot.

Halachic — The adjective form of halacha.

Hashem — Translates from Hebrew to mean "The Name" and is commonly used in conversation by observant Jews to substitute for the word *God*.

Kabbalist — A practitioner or teacher of Kabbalah, a component of Judaism that conveys hidden and mystical tenets integral to a more complete connection and understanding of God.

Kiddush Hashem   Literally means "sanctification of The Name." Practically means something done to glorify or bring honor to God.

Mensch   A Yiddish term meaning a real gentleman, a great guy. Can also be used to describe a woman, equally as complimentary but not used as often.

Meshugass   Craziness.

Mikveh   A bath or special body of water used for ritual immersion.

Minyan   A quorum of ten adult Jewish males required to be able to read from the Torah.

Mitzvah   Loosely translated as a good deed, but more accurately, a specific commandment from God. Plural is mitzvoth.

Mohel   A Jewish man trained in the ritual and procedure required to do a bris.

Neshama   Name for the Jewish soul

Oedipal Complex   A concept developed by Sigmund Freud to explain unconscious wishes, fantasies, and behaviors in children, the ramifications of which can be seen in adults by astute psychiatrists or sophisticated comedians.

Parsha   A chapter in the Torah

Pidyon Haben   Translates to "redemption of the firstborn." Just as it was done in the time of Aaron, a young Jewish boy is redeemed from the High Priest, or today his descendent or Kohanim, for silver coins.

Seder   A festive, joyous meal during Passover, accompanied by prayer and retelling the story of the Jew's exodus from Egypt.

Shabbos   Ashkenazic pronunciation of Shabbat, or the day of rest, which runs from approximately eighteen minutes before sundown on Friday to about forty-five minutes after sundown on Saturday.

Shema   Centerpiece of a Jewish prayer service, calling for all of Israel to acknowledge the one God.

Shaliach   Loosely translated as "messenger." Commonly used to describe the young men or women of Chabad who leave Crown Heights to go out and spread the good word.

Shul   Yiddish word for synagogue.

Sandek   Honor that is given to someone at a bris who holds the baby during or just after the procedure.

Simon tov oo mazel tov   Most of the words of a cute little song sung in celebration at a Jewish event.

String Theory   The concept in physics attempting to unify quantum mechanics and general relativity. For whatever it's worth, many of the big players in this field seem to be Jewish.

Tallit   A Jewish prayer shawl.

Talmud	The Oral Law passed down through the generations from the time of Moses until written down in approximately 200 CE.
Teshuva	The root of the word means "to return." It is the process of repentance to God or a fellow human being.
Tefillin	Two small boxes with leather straps that are attached to the arm and head of a Jewish male during morning prayers.
Tzadik	A righteous or holy person.
Tzedakah	Commonly means charity. From the same root as tzadik, so it also means righteousness.
Tzitzit	Four fringes with knots on the corners of a garment worn by Jewish men.
Yiddishkeit lifestyle.	Commonly used to mean Jewish

Dr. Fine lives, practices and davens in
Vacaville, California.

Made in the USA
Middletown, DE
24 June 2023

33214619R10066